EMMANUEL JOSEPH

Green Pixel Wardrobe, The Future of Digital Fashion

Copyright © 2025 by Emmanuel Joseph

All rights reserved. No part of this publication may be reproduced, stored or transmitted in any form or by any means, electronic, mechanical, photocopying, recording, scanning, or otherwise without written permission from the publisher. It is illegal to copy this book, post it to a website, or distribute it by any other means without permission.

First edition

This book was professionally typeset on Reedsy.
Find out more at reedsy.com

Contents

1	Chapter 1: The Evolution of Fashion	1
2	Chapter 2: The Birth of Digital Fashion	3
3	Chapter 3: Virtual Wardrobes	5
4	Chapter 4: The Role of Augmented Reality	7
5	Chapter 5: The Impact on Sustainability	9
6	Chapter 6: Fashion in the Metaverse	11
7	Chapter 7: The Role of Blockchain	13
8	Chapter 8: Digital Fashion Brands	15
9	Chapter 9: The Future of Fashion Retail	17
10	Chapter 10: Fashion and Gaming	19
11	Chapter 11: Fashion Designers in the Digital Age	21
12	Chapter 12: The Social Media Influence	23
13	Chapter 13: Customization and Personalization	25
14	Chapter 14: Challenges and Controversies	27
15	Chapter 15: The Future of Digital Fashion	29

1

Chapter 1: The Evolution of Fashion

Fashion has always been a reflection of society's evolving tastes, values, and technological advancements. From the ornate garments of ancient civilizations to the minimalist designs of the 21st century, clothing has consistently mirrored the zeitgeist of the times. But now, as we stand on the brink of a digital revolution, the future of fashion promises to be unlike anything we've seen before.

In the bustling city of Florence during the Renaissance, the Medici family's opulent attire was a symbol of their power and influence. Their richly embroidered robes and intricate jewelry were not just expressions of wealth but also of the cultural renaissance that was sweeping across Europe. Fast forward to the 1960s, and the world witnessed a fashion revolution of a different kind. The streets of London became a runway for the bold and eclectic styles of the mod subculture, which rejected the conservative norms of the previous decade.

Today, fashion is entering a new era—one that transcends the physical world and ventures into the digital realm. Imagine a wardrobe that exists entirely in the virtual space, where garments can change color and style with a simple swipe. In this chapter, we'll explore the historical journey of fashion and set the stage for the digital transformation that is about to unfold.

Let's take a step back in time to understand how we've arrived at this pivotal moment. In the early 2000s, the fashion industry began experimenting with digital tools and techniques. Designers used 3D modeling software to create virtual prototypes of their collections, allowing them to visualize and perfect their designs before producing a single garment. This was just the beginning. As technology continued to advance, so did the possibilities for digital fashion.

One of the pioneers in this field was Clara Roberts, a young designer from New York who saw the potential of combining her love for fashion with her passion for technology. Clara's groundbreaking collection, "Virtual Vogue," debuted in 2010 and featured garments that existed solely in the digital realm. Using a blend of augmented reality (AR) and virtual reality (VR), Clara created an immersive fashion experience that captivated audiences worldwide.

2

Chapter 2: The Birth of Digital Fashion

The birth of digital fashion is a story of creativity, innovation, and the fusion of two worlds—technology and art. It wasn't a sudden event but rather a gradual evolution driven by visionaries who saw the potential of virtual clothing long before it became a trend.

In the late 2000s, a group of forward-thinking designers began experimenting with digital tools to create virtual garments. Among them was Clara Roberts, a young designer from New York who had a knack for blending technology with fashion. Her debut collection, "Virtual Vogue," showcased garments that existed solely in the digital realm. Using augmented reality (AR) and virtual reality (VR), Clara created an immersive fashion experience that captivated audiences worldwide.

Clara's success inspired other designers to explore the possibilities of digital fashion. One such designer was Hiroshi Tanaka from Tokyo, who believed that virtual clothing could revolutionize the fashion industry. Hiroshi's innovative approach involved using 3D modeling software to create intricate and customizable digital garments. His collections quickly gained popularity, and he became a leading figure in the world of digital fashion.

As the technology behind digital fashion continued to advance, so did the possibilities for virtual wardrobes. Designers began experimenting with new materials, textures, and designs that were impossible to achieve with physical fabrics. This newfound freedom allowed for unprecedented creativity and innovation.

The rise of social media platforms further fueled the growth of digital fashion. Influencers and celebrities began showcasing virtual garments in their posts, setting trends and shaping consumer behavior. The digital fashion community grew rapidly, and soon, virtual clothing became a mainstream phenomenon.

3

Chapter 3: Virtual Wardrobes

Imagine a world where your wardrobe exists entirely in the digital realm. No more cluttered closets or laundry days. Instead, you have an infinite selection of outfits that can be customized in real-time. This chapter explores the concept of virtual wardrobes and the technology behind them.

In the year 2025, Sarah Mitchell, a fashion enthusiast from Los Angeles, wakes up to find herself in a futuristic world where virtual wardrobes are the norm. With a simple swipe on her smart mirror, she can access an array of digital garments, each one perfectly tailored to her taste and body shape. Sarah's virtual wardrobe is connected to her social media profiles, allowing her to share her outfits with friends and followers instantly.

The technology behind virtual wardrobes is a marvel of modern innovation. Using advanced 3D modeling software, designers create digital garments that are indistinguishable from physical clothing. These garments can be customized in real-time, allowing users to change colors, patterns, and styles with ease. Augmented reality (AR) technology enables users to see themselves in their virtual outfits, blending the physical and digital worlds seamlessly.

One of the pioneers in virtual wardrobe technology is Dr. Elena Martínez, a computer scientist from Spain who developed a groundbreaking algorithm for creating realistic digital fabrics. Her work revolutionized the digital fashion industry, making virtual wardrobes more accessible and user-friendly.

Virtual wardrobes offer numerous benefits beyond just convenience. They promote sustainability by reducing the need for physical clothing production and minimizing waste. They also provide a platform for creative expression, allowing users to experiment with different styles and designs without the limitations of physical fabrics.

4

Chapter 4: The Role of Augmented Reality

Augmented reality (AR) is a key player in the world of digital fashion. It allows users to see themselves in virtual garments, blending the physical and digital worlds. We'll explore how AR is transforming the fashion industry and providing new opportunities for self-expression.

In the bustling streets of Seoul, fashion-forward individuals can be seen wearing AR glasses that project virtual garments onto their bodies. These glasses are equipped with advanced sensors and cameras that capture the user's movements and environment, creating a seamless blend of reality and virtuality. For instance, Ji-ho Kim, a young artist, uses AR glasses to create stunning visual art pieces that incorporate virtual fashion elements.

AR technology is also transforming the shopping experience. In Milan, a high-end boutique offers an AR-powered fitting room where customers can try on virtual garments before making a purchase. This not only enhances the shopping experience but also reduces the need for physical samples, leading to a more sustainable fashion industry.

Fashion designers are embracing AR technology to push the boundaries of creativity. Take the case of Alexei Volkov, a Russian designer known for his futuristic and avant-garde designs. Using AR, Alexei creates virtual fashion shows where models walk the runway in digital garments that change in real-time based on audience feedback. This interactive and immersive experience captivates viewers and sets a new standard for fashion shows.

The integration of AR in digital fashion is opening up new avenues for self-expression. Users can experiment with different styles, colors, and patterns without the limitations of physical fabrics. AR also allows for real-time customization, enabling individuals to create unique and personalized looks that reflect their personality and taste.

5

Chapter 5: The Impact on Sustainability

Digital fashion offers a more sustainable alternative to traditional clothing. With no physical production, it reduces waste and minimizes environmental impact. We'll discuss the environmental benefits of digital fashion and how it aligns with the growing demand for eco-friendly solutions.

In a world increasingly aware of its environmental footprint, digital fashion presents a promising solution. The traditional fashion industry is notorious for its high levels of waste and pollution, from textile production to garment disposal. Digital fashion, on the other hand, eliminates the need for physical fabrics, dyes, and production processes, significantly reducing its environmental impact.

Take the example of Lisa Thompson, a sustainability advocate from London. Lisa's wardrobe is entirely digital, with each garment designed to be worn in virtual environments. By embracing digital fashion, Lisa has drastically reduced her carbon footprint and supports brands that prioritize eco-friendly practices.

Digital fashion also addresses the issue of fast fashion. In the physical world, trends come and go, leading to a cycle of constant consumption and waste. With virtual garments, users can easily update their wardrobe to keep up with the latest trends without contributing to environmental degradation. This shift towards digital fashion promotes a more sustainable and mindful approach to clothing.

The rise of digital fashion has also led to the emergence of eco-conscious designers like Ayesha Patel from Mumbai. Ayesha's virtual collections are inspired by nature and incorporate sustainable design principles. By creating digital garments that mimic natural textures and patterns, Ayesha raises awareness about the importance of preserving our planet's resources.

Furthermore, digital fashion offers a solution to the problem of overproduction. In traditional fashion, unsold inventory often ends up in landfills, contributing to environmental pollution. With virtual garments, there is no need for physical production, storage, or disposal. This not only reduces waste but also aligns with the growing demand for sustainable and ethical fashion practices.

6

Chapter 6: Fashion in the Metaverse

The metaverse is a virtual universe where digital fashion thrives. In this chapter, we'll explore the possibilities of fashion in the metaverse, from virtual runway shows to immersive shopping experiences. The line between reality and virtuality is becoming increasingly blurred.

In the bustling metaverse city of Neotopia, fashion enthusiasts gather for the annual Virtual Fashion Week. Avatars strut down the runway in breathtaking digital garments, showcasing the latest creations from renowned designers. The audience, composed of avatars from around the world, watches in awe as the virtual garments change color and shape in real-time.

One of the highlights of Virtual Fashion Week is the debut collection by Zara Li, a digital fashion designer from Shanghai. Zara's collection, "Ethereal Dreams," features garments that defy the laws of physics, with flowing textures and shimmering colors that seem to dance in the air. The virtual runway show is an immersive experience, with holographic projections and interactive elements that captivate the audience.

The metaverse also offers unique shopping experiences. In the virtual shopping district of Luxora, users can visit digital boutiques and try on virtual garments using augmented reality (AR) technology. These boutiques are designed to be visually stunning, with futuristic architecture and dynamic displays that showcase the latest trends. Customers can customize their virtual outfits and make instant purchases, receiving their digital garments in seconds.

Fashion in the metaverse is not limited by the constraints of the physical world. Designers can experiment with innovative materials, shapes, and designs that would be impossible to achieve in reality. This freedom of creativity has led to the emergence of avant-garde fashion brands like Neon Couture, known for their bold and futuristic virtual garments.

The metaverse also provides a platform for fashion communities to connect and collaborate. In the virtual city of Novus, fashion enthusiasts participate in virtual styling competitions, where they create unique looks using digital garments. These competitions foster a sense of community and encourage creative expression, allowing individuals to showcase their style and gain recognition in the digital fashion world.

7

Chapter 7: The Role of Blockchain

Blockchain technology plays a crucial role in digital fashion, providing security and authenticity. It ensures that virtual garments are unique and cannot be duplicated. We'll delve into the intersection of fashion and blockchain, highlighting its importance in the digital age.

In the digital fashion industry, the issue of authenticity is paramount. Virtual garments, like physical ones, need to be protected from counterfeiting and duplication. This is where blockchain technology comes into play. By creating a decentralized and immutable ledger, blockchain ensures that each digital garment is unique and verifiable.

Let's take the example of Elena Novak, a digital fashion designer from Prague. Elena's virtual garments are renowned for their intricate designs and high quality. To protect her creations, she uses blockchain technology to create a digital certificate of authenticity for each garment. This certificate, stored on the blockchain, verifies the garment's origin and ownership, ensuring that it cannot be duplicated or counterfeited.

Blockchain also facilitates secure transactions in the digital fashion industry. In the virtual marketplace of Vynex, users can buy, sell, and trade digital garments with confidence. Each transaction is recorded on the blockchain, providing a transparent and tamper-proof record of ownership. This not only ensures the blockchain technology provides a secure and transparent platform for the digital fashion industry, it also enables the creation of unique and limited-edition virtual garments. Designers can release exclusive collections, with each garment being a one-of-a-kind piece, verified by the blockchain. This not only adds value to the digital fashion market but also encourages creativity and innovation.

One notable example is the collaboration between digital fashion designer Nadia Amari and a blockchain platform called EtherWardrobe. Nadia's collection, "Digital Couture," features limited-edition virtual garments, each accompanied by a digital certificate of authenticity. These certificates are stored on the blockchain, ensuring the uniqueness and provenance of each piece. The collection quickly gained popularity, with fashion enthusiasts eagerly participating in online auctions to own a piece of digital couture.

Blockchain technology also facilitates the resale of digital garments. In the virtual marketplace of Vynex, users can buy, sell, and trade virtual clothing with confidence. Each transaction is recorded on the blockchain, providing a transparent and tamper-proof record of ownership. This not only ensures the authenticity of the garments but also creates a thriving secondary market for digital fashion.

8

Chapter 8: Digital Fashion Brands

A new wave of fashion brands is emerging in the digital space. These brands are breaking away from traditional norms and embracing the limitless possibilities of virtual clothing. This chapter introduces some of the most innovative digital fashion brands and their unique offerings.

One of the trailblazers in the digital fashion industry is Neon Couture, a brand known for its bold and futuristic designs. Founded by visionary designer Zara Li, Neon Couture has quickly become a favorite among fashion enthusiasts in the metaverse. Zara's collections feature garments that defy the laws of physics, with holographic textures and dynamic shapes that change in real time.

Another prominent digital fashion brand is Pixel Threads, founded by tech-savvy designer Alexei Volkov. Pixel Threads specializes in customizable virtual garments, allowing users to personalize their outfits with unique colors, patterns, and accessories. Alexei's innovative approach has made Pixel Threads a popular choice for those looking to express their individuality in the digital realm.

EcoVogue is a digital fashion brand that prioritizes sustainability and eco-conscious design. Founded by Ayesha Patel, EcoVogue's collections are inspired by nature and incorporate sustainable design principles. Ayesha's virtual garments mimic natural textures and patterns, raising awareness about the importance of preserving our planet's resources.

These digital fashion brands are redefining the fashion landscape, offering consumers a new way to experience and interact with clothing. By embracing technology and innovation, they are paving the way for the future of fashion.

9

Chapter 9: The Future of Fashion Retail

The retail landscape is evolving, with digital fashion leading the way. From virtual boutiques to personalized shopping experiences, the future of fashion retail is here. We'll explore how digital fashion is transforming the retail industry and what it means for consumers.

In the virtual shopping district of Luxora, customers can visit digital boutiques and explore a wide range of virtual garments. These boutiques are designed to be visually stunning, with futuristic architecture and dynamic displays that showcase the latest trends. Using augmented reality (AR) technology, customers can try on virtual outfits and see how they look before making a purchase.

One of the pioneers in digital fashion retail is StyloSphere, a virtual boutique that offers personalized shopping experiences. Founded by fashion entrepreneur Elena Martínez, StyloSphere uses advanced AI algorithms to analyze customer preferences and recommend outfits tailored to their taste. Customers can interact with virtual fashion consultants and receive real-time styling advice, enhancing the overall shopping experience.

The rise of digital fashion has also led to the emergence of pop-up virtual stores. These temporary stores appear in the metaverse for a limited time, offering exclusive collections and limited-edition garments. Fashion enthusiasts eagerly anticipate these pop-up events, which often feature interactive elements and immersive experiences.

Digital fashion retail is not limited by geographical boundaries. Customers from around the world can access virtual boutiques and purchase digital garments with ease. This global accessibility has opened up new markets and opportunities for fashion brands, allowing them to reach a broader audience.

10

Chapter 10: Fashion and Gaming

The gaming industry has long been a pioneer in digital fashion. Avatars in video games often wear elaborate outfits that can be customized by players. This chapter explores the crossover between fashion and gaming and how it has influenced the rise of digital fashion.

In the vibrant world of online gaming, avatars are a powerful form of self-expression. Players spend hours customizing their avatars with unique outfits, accessories, and hairstyles, reflecting their personality and style. Games like "Fashion Fantasy" and "Virtual Vogue" have become popular platforms for digital fashion enthusiasts, offering a wide range of virtual garments and styling options.

One of the most influential figures in the gaming and fashion crossover is Hiroshi Tanaka, a renowned game designer and digital fashion pioneer. Hiroshi's game "Fashion Quest" allows players to embark on a virtual adventure, collecting rare and exclusive virtual garments along the way. The game's immersive storyline and stunning visuals have captivated millions of players, making it a cultural phenomenon.

The collaboration between fashion brands and gaming companies has further fueled the growth of digital fashion. In 2023, luxury fashion house Maison de Couture partnered with the popular game "Avatar Universe" to release a limited-edition collection of virtual garments. Players could purchase these exclusive outfits for their avatars, blending the worlds of high fashion and gaming.

The influence of gaming on digital fashion is evident in the rise of virtual fashion shows and competitions within the gaming community. Players participate in virtual runway events, showcasing their avatars in elaborate digital garments. These events foster creativity and innovation, pushing the boundaries of digital fashion and inspiring new trends.

11

Chapter 11: Fashion Designers in the Digital Age

The role of fashion designers is evolving in the digital age. They are no longer limited by physical constraints and can let their creativity run wild. We'll highlight some of the most innovative digital fashion designers and their contributions to the industry.

One of the most celebrated digital fashion designers is Clara Roberts, whose groundbreaking collection "Virtual Vogue" set the stage for the digital fashion revolution. Clara's innovative use of augmented reality (AR) and virtual reality (VR) technology allowed her to create immersive fashion experiences that captivated audiences worldwide.

Another prominent figure in the digital fashion industry is Alexei Volkov, the founder of Pixel Threads. Alexei's customizable virtual garments have gained a loyal following, with users embracing the opportunity to express their individuality through personalized outfits. His innovative designs have redefined the concept of fashion in the digital realm.

Ayesha Patel, the founder of EcoVogue, is a pioneer in sustainable digital fashion. Her collections are inspired by nature and incorporate eco-conscious design principles. Ayesha's virtual garments raise awareness about environmental preservation and promote a more sustainable approach to fashion.

Zara Li, the visionary behind Neon Couture, is known for her bold and futuristic designs. Zara's virtual garments defy the laws of physics, with holographic textures and dynamic shapes that change in real time. Her collections have become a favorite among fashion enthusiasts in the metaverse.

These designers are pushing the boundaries of creativity and innovation, redefining what it means to be a fashion designer in the digital age. By embracing technology and exploring new possibilities, they are shaping the future of fashion.

12

Chapter 12: The Social Media Influence

Social media platforms are a powerful tool for promoting digital fashion. Influencers and celebrities are often seen wearing virtual garments, setting trends and shaping consumer behavior. This chapter delves into the role of social media in the rise of digital fashion.

In the world of social media, visual content reigns supreme. Platforms like Instagram, TikTok, and Pinterest have become essential for fashion influencers and brands to showcase their latest creations. Virtual garments, with their eye-catching designs and interactive elements, are perfectly suited for the digital age.

Influencers like Mia Johnson, a digital fashion icon from Los Angeles, have gained massive followings by embracing virtual clothing. Mia's Instagram feed is a kaleidoscope of vibrant colors and futuristic designs, featuring virtual garments from top digital fashion brands. Her followers eagerly await her posts, drawing inspiration from her unique style and creative outfits.

The rise of social media has also given birth to virtual influencers—digital personas created by designers and AI developers. One such virtual influencer is Lila Grace, a virtual model with millions of followers on Instagram. Lila's lifelike appearance and captivating fashion sense have made her a sensation, blurring the lines between reality and virtuality.

Fashion brands are leveraging social media to engage with their audience and promote their virtual collections. Interactive features like AR filters and virtual try-ons allow users to experience digital fashion in a fun and engaging way. Brands like Neon Couture and Pixel Threads use social media campaigns to showcase their latest designs and connect with fashion enthusiasts worldwide.

The influence of social media on digital fashion is undeniable. It has democratized the fashion industry, giving a platform to emerging designers and allowing consumers to discover new trends and styles. As social media continues to evolve, it will play an increasingly important role in the growth of digital fashion.

13

Chapter 13: Customization and Personalization

Digital fashion offers unparalleled opportunities for customization and personalization. Users can design their own virtual garments and express their unique style. We'll explore the tools and technologies that make this possible and how they are changing the fashion landscape.

In the digital fashion world, creativity knows no bounds. Advanced 3D modeling software and design tools allow users to create bespoke virtual garments tailored to their preferences. Whether it's changing colors, patterns, or adding unique accessories, the possibilities for customization are endless.

Take the example of Emma Davis, a fashion enthusiast from Sydney. Emma uses a digital fashion app called StyleMe, which allows her to design her own virtual outfits. With a simple drag-and-drop interface, she can mix and match different elements to create unique looks that reflect her personality and style. Emma's virtual wardrobe is a testament to her creativity, featuring a diverse range of customized virtual garments. Emma's journey in digital fashion is a testament to the power of customization and how it allows individuals to express their unique style.

Digital fashion platforms like FashionFusion and StyleMe are revolutionizing the way users interact with clothing. These platforms offer intuitive design tools, allowing users to create and modify virtual garments with ease. From selecting fabrics and colors to adding intricate patterns and embellishments, the possibilities for customization are endless.

One of the most exciting aspects of digital fashion is the ability to create one-of-a-kind pieces. Users can design garments that are tailored to their preferences and reflect their personal style. This level of customization fosters creativity and individuality, allowing fashion enthusiasts to stand out in the digital realm.

Fashion designers are also leveraging customization to create interactive and engaging experiences for their customers. In the virtual boutique of Pixel Threads, customers can collaborate with designers to create bespoke virtual garments. This personalized approach enhances the customer experience and builds a strong connection between the brand and its audience.

Customization and personalization are not limited to individual users. Digital fashion brands are exploring innovative ways to offer tailored experiences to their customers. For example, EcoVogue offers a customization feature that allows users to select eco-friendly materials and designs inspired by nature. This aligns with the brand's commitment to sustainability and provides a unique and meaningful experience for customers.

14

Chapter 14: Challenges and Controversies

Like any industry, digital fashion faces its own set of challenges and controversies. From issues of copyright and ownership to the digital divide, we'll discuss the hurdles that need to be addressed for digital fashion to thrive.

One of the primary challenges in the digital fashion industry is the issue of copyright and ownership. As virtual garments become more popular, the risk of duplication and piracy increases. Designers invest significant time and effort into creating unique digital pieces, and protecting their intellectual property is crucial. Blockchain technology offers a solution by providing a secure and transparent platform for verifying the authenticity of virtual garments. However, the implementation and adoption of blockchain across the industry remain a challenge.

Another challenge is the digital divide, which refers to the gap between individuals who have access to digital technology and those who do not. Digital fashion relies heavily on advanced technology, and individuals without access to these tools may be excluded from participating in the digital fashion revolution. Bridging this gap requires investment in digital infrastructure and initiatives to promote digital literacy.

The environmental impact of digital technology is also a concern. While digital fashion offers a more sustainable alternative to traditional clothing, the energy consumption of data centers and digital platforms cannot be overlooked. It is essential for the industry to adopt eco-friendly practices and explore renewable energy sources to minimize its environmental footprint.

The rise of digital fashion has also sparked debates about body image and inclusivity. Virtual garments can be tailored to fit any body type, but there is a risk of perpetuating unrealistic beauty standards. Designers and brands must prioritize inclusivity and represent diverse body shapes and sizes in their virtual collections.

Despite these challenges, the digital fashion industry holds immense potential for innovation and growth. By addressing these hurdles and embracing ethical and sustainable practices, digital fashion can continue to thrive and revolutionize the way we interact with clothing.

15

Chapter 15: The Future of Digital Fashion

As we look to the future, digital fashion is poised to become an integral part of our lives. This chapter envisions what the future holds for digital fashion and its potential to revolutionize the way we express ourselves through clothing.

In the not-so-distant future, digital fashion will be seamlessly integrated into our daily lives. Smart mirrors equipped with augmented reality (AR) technology will allow us to try on virtual garments with ease. Virtual wardrobes will offer an infinite selection of outfits, personalized to our preferences and tailored to our body shapes.

The metaverse will continue to evolve, providing a vibrant and dynamic platform for digital fashion. Virtual fashion shows and immersive shopping experiences will become the norm, allowing fashion enthusiasts to explore and interact with clothing in new and exciting ways. The line between reality and virtuality will become increasingly blurred, offering endless possibilities for creative expression.

Digital fashion will also play a significant role in promoting sustainability and eco-conscious practices. With no physical production, virtual garments will reduce waste and minimize environmental impact. Brands will prioritize ethical and sustainable design principles, creating virtual collections that raise awareness about environmental preservation.

The future of digital fashion will be driven by innovation and technology. Advanced AI algorithms will enable hyper-personalized shopping experiences, recommending outfits tailored to our tastes and preferences. Blockchain technology will ensure the authenticity and uniqueness of virtual garments, creating a secure and transparent marketplace for digital fashion.

As we embrace the digital fashion revolution, we will discover new ways to express ourselves through clothing. Virtual garments will become a canvas for creativity, allowing us to experiment with styles, colors, and designs without limitations. The future of digital fashion is bright, and it promises to transform the way we perceive and interact with clothing.

Description: Green Pixel Wardrobe: The Future of Digital Fashion

Step into the captivating world of **"Green Pixel Wardrobe: The Future of Digital Fashion,"** a groundbreaking exploration of the digital transformation in the fashion industry. This thrilling book delves into the revolutionary shift from traditional clothing to virtual garments, offering readers a glimpse into the future of fashion.

Journey through the pages as we uncover the origins of digital fashion and the visionary pioneers who made it possible. Discover the marvels of virtual wardrobes and the role of augmented reality (AR) in creating immersive fashion experiences. Learn how digital fashion aligns with sustainability efforts and promises a more eco-friendly alternative to physical clothing.

Venture into the metaverse, where fashion thrives in a virtual universe, and explore the fusion of fashion and blockchain technology, ensuring the authenticity and uniqueness of virtual garments. Meet the innovative digital fashion brands and designers who are pushing the boundaries of creativity and redefining the industry.

Experience the future of fashion retail with virtual boutiques, personalized shopping experiences, and the influence of social media in shaping trends and consumer behavior. Delve into the exciting crossover between fashion and gaming, where avatars become powerful forms of self-expression.

With a perfect blend of fascinating stories, cutting-edge technology, and visionary insights, **"Green Pixel Wardrobe: The Future of Digital Fashion"** is an engaging and thought-provoking read for fashion enthusiasts, tech aficionados, and anyone curious about the future of clothing. Get ready to

CHAPTER 15: THE FUTURE OF DIGITAL FASHION

embark on an unforgettable journey into the world of digital fashion and discover how it will revolutionize the way we express ourselves through clothing.

www.ingramcontent.com/pod-product-compliance
Lightning Source LLC
LaVergne TN
LVHW020502080526
838202LV00057B/6101